another beginning

another beginning

poems by

caitlin blackburn

Antrim House
Bloomfield, Connecticut

Library of Congress Control Number: 2022915856

ISBN: 979-8-9855621-9-4

First Edition

Printed & bound by Ingram Content Group

Book design by Rennie McQuilkin

Front cover photograph by Gak Stonn

Author photograph by Marisa Garcia

Antrim House
860.217.0023
AntrimHouseBooks@gmail.com
www.AntrimHouseBooks.com
400 Seabury Dr., #5196, Bloomfield, CT 06002

for all of my compassionate witnesses
who never let me abandon myself:
thank you for seeing me.

table of contents

whatever
returns from oblivion returns
to find a voice.

– louise glück

another beginning

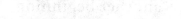

prelude

on the last day, before the beginning of it all
the girl crawled for miles until she reached the edge.

covered in dirt and bleeding from her palms and her knees
she screamed into the vast universe, begging it to swallow her whole.

but the universe said, "no, you need to carry on."
the girl writhed with a pain so intense she was sure her heart was
breaking apart.

she didn't want to carry on, so why couldn't she force herself over
into the abyss?

maybe because, on the last day before the beginning of it all, that
vast universe picked her up and held her,
keeping her safe from herself.

and in the morning, on the first day of the beginning of it all
the girl looked at where she had come from – the path covered in
blood and tears – and then she chose to go another way.

so, she walked. on a path that had never been walked upon before.
the ground cut her feet and the branches whipped at her legs, but
she continued on – and some of the walls she had built around her
heart began to crack and fall.

and then, some light began to come into her heart.
the girl had forgotten what that warmth felt like – it filled her with
an unfamiliar joy that made her weep.

"no more!" she whispered to herself as she wrapped herself in her
own embrace.

and another wall around her heart collapsed.

and so she continued on, though the way was treacherous
and uncertain,
because she saw no reason to return to the place she had been
on the last day, before the beginning of it all.

1. the parting

i am out with lanterns, looking for myself.

−emily dickinson

I

there was a time when i believed that time healed all wounds.
so i gathered the broken pieces and hid them away,
biding my time.
but time did not heal.
time eroded.

II

i don't know when i gave up trying to take root.
but i grew tired
of being tended to,
of being exceedingly temperamental,
of being watched so closely,
all in the hope i would establish myself,
even if only for a season.

i was made to be wild.
not violently ripped from the ground too early,
taken from where i belonged,
and forced to be an accessory.
i was never meant to be here – can't you see!
so let me rest
and stop expecting a miracle.

each time you see me bow my head towards the earth – wilting,
know that i'm finding peace.
i don't want to be revived.
i long to be starved of all that nourishes me
and to die in the dark home i've created.
because soon you will understand that,
without me your world can be beautiful again.

III

nothing is real – nothing is true
we are all just playing dress-up in the dark.
hoping no one sees us for who we truly are
yet dying to be seen.
dying to be heard.

i would cry out
but i've already swallowed every word
and those words, they're infecting me
preventing me from truly living.

white knuckles gripping onto this life
begging for a reprieve
which only comes when the mask is on.
so glorious and magnificent – i can almost convince myself
it's true.

but i'm living in dust and shadows,
immeasurable obscurity.
i know that with all of this darkness outside of me
there is still so much more within.

and to survive
nothing can be real, nothing can be true
because to survive
we can't be seen
and we can't be heard –

we just need to keep playing dress-up in the dark.

IV

i want to bury it all.
push it far into the ground.
a seedling
i'll never nourish.
deeper and deeper
until it doesn't exist to me.
and still,
like a weed
it pushes through the earth
unwanted
and ugly.
i rip it from the ground
trying to take the roots.
but only the stems free themselves.

V

pushing
pushing pushing
it all past the periphery
out of sight
out of mind
out of heart
and spirit
and existence
but only for a moment
because
with the turn of a head
it all comes into focus
sharper than ever
a reminder of why it was pushed so far
away in the first place.

VI

if only i were someone else
rather than just a bystander
seeing all of what i could have been
if i could have just removed myself
from my own thoughts.
i'm all of the things i never wished to be
and now,
it's all habit
ingrained in every cell.
there is no changing
or pulling it apart.
there is no revealing
a diamond in the rough.
i can never be shiny, or new, or spectacular.
i am only what i am.
i am only everything
i ever feared i'd become.
and i push against it
with all of my might
in the hopes of putting some distance between it and me.
but it never budges.
not even the smallest bit.
i'm confined to all i figured i would be.
perhaps that was all by design.
perhaps it was of my own making,
my own plans
to never be anything more
than my biggest fears
and my ugly truths.
to keep me small and safe
until my soul was exhausted
and ready to move on.

VII

all of the thoughts colliding
in the container of my mind.
controlling everything but my heart
who waits quietly
for me to ask her for the answers.
sweet,
tender love
waiting for me.
but the mind is a maze
and i'm lost in its darkest corners.
afraid to venture forward
afraid to seek out the light.
the sharp edges of my own thoughts
press themselves into my progress
and weaken my resolve
until i'm compliant,
until i'm full agreement,
until i'm a co-conspirator.

my voice.
if only i could use my voice,
that beautiful bridge to my heart.
but i'm silent.
terrified and unsure
to fully express
the depth of my own predicament.
i wish to remain "normal"
and "healed"
and "an inspiration."
but i'm not so inspiring now,
not while i'm under the spell of my own saboteur.
under duress

i obey her
despite knowing
there has to be another way out.
but in this moment there is no trace of light to guide me
and i feel i might finally be lost forever.

VIII

i feel and i write
i write best when i'm depressed.

so they tell me to put down my pen,
stop expressing what's in my heart,
that i'll just send myself further into a spiral –
my scars are not some type of art.

but i want to show you
want you to know
that all of this pain pent up inside of me
needs someplace to go.

it's like a poison.
i don't know how to make you see
that holding it all in
is slowly killing me.

IX

through the storm i heard them –
the voices saying what they've always said
as if there was nothing else to say.
the footsteps trampling the paths they've always trampled
as if there was no place else to go.
and they trapped me
by eliminating the periphery
so that all i could see was what they wanted me to see –
a narrow view
constructed without my input.
i did not consent to being too much.
i did not consent to being not enough.
i did not consent
and now
i am unrecognizable.

X

and in the remembering
it's glassy eyes,
a dry throat
and suffocated lungs
all giving way to choked words.
two people
completely tethered together
in this life and the next.
all shame and frozen features.
a brain disconnected from a body.
words will never be enough
to describe it in its entirety.
but the remembering,
the reliving
is an imprint on the soul.

XI

silence.
even writing the words feels too loud
so i pause,
i refrain –

they don't hear me anyway,
raw and vulnerable.
they can't see me.
a scream or a whisper,
it doesn't matter –

the words become lost,
dissolving into the winter air,
gone
like they never existed at all.

and i question . . .
maybe it's their ears, their hearts and their minds –
maybe it's not me at all.

the words are crystal clear
yet they get distorted and smudged
like fingerprints on a glass –

everything looks different,
everything sounds different.

so silence is where i land,
choking myself to protect myself.
they tell me i'm crazy
but i've learned
this is the only way to keep myself safe.

XII

it all hurt – so i had to disengage from it.
staring off into nothingness, all while trying to pretend i was still inside,
i was still present.

wasn't i?
but no.
i had drifted somewhere far away, the sound of her voice becoming muffled.
as if i had slipped under water.
stillness.

but i had to hold my breath.

i thought you could die in the disconnection – if there's nothing to bring you back.
after all, you can only stay underwater for so long.
you either have to reach the surface or surrender to the drowning.
so i reach the surface.

the world, even brighter and louder than i remembered it.
her voice isn't muffled anymore
and it hurts –

the words she is choosing to say.
i notice
i am still holding my breath – WHY AM I HOLDING MY BREATH!?
coming to the surface made no difference.

this twisted knot in my abdomen is fighting to untie itself
but i am not safe enough to let it.

if i exhale, everything will unravel.
if i allow myself to breathe,
i will scream.
and truth be told, i'm probably just being dramatic.

dramatic – that word bounces around my brain as if my skull
is a pinball machine.
it's loud and persistent. relentless.
i slip back below the surface.
calm and quiet again.
and then i realize
it doesn't matter where i go – i'll always have to hold my breath.

XIII

eyes wide open –
it isn't safe, my dear.
i know you're tired of the night,
kept awake by fear.

the mind swirls in the shadows
dredging up all of the ways you are wrong
but you cannot look away –
you've been in danger far too long.

wrap your arms around yourself
to create the illusion of control
and stop wondering about what could have been –
you'll never recover what they stole.

you will always be just a child
incurably afraid of the dark,
constantly remembering
that night you lost your spark.

so force yourself to stay awake
and don't forget to stay alert
because you wouldn't be feeling the way you are now
if you hadn't let yourself get hurt.

XIV

i told myself
i would awaken
at the first sign of spring.
that i would locate the joy again
and that my heart would sing once more.
i hear the birds
outside of my window
calling to me,
"spring is here."
i see the morning sunlight
flooding the bedroom
beckoning me
to emerge.
i recall the oath
i swore to myself
in the depths of winter
but i close the blinds anyway
and cover my ears.
promises i make to myself
are rarely kept.
maybe the next season will be better.

XV

words –
where are the words
to describe
the emptiness
and disconnection
so deeply contained
within this body?
they swell within me,
an edema pressing
against the boundary
of my muscles,
tendons,
skin,
and bones.
i could burst –
a literal floodgate
giving way
so i spill all over the floor.
my emptiness pouring out
and seeping into the carpet.
is that death,
when everything within me
becomes without?
or is that freedom?
or maybe
it's both.

XVI

bone-shattering cold
permeates me.
the wind
blows so hard that i cannot hear anything.
my thoughts feel like they're screaming
just to be heard.
the salty spray from the waves
stings my face.
am i crying?
or is this just rain and sea?
i might laugh
if this didn't seem like such a punishment.
somehow i let myself get strangled
by my own rigidity.

XVII

i'm tangled up
with the strings
so tightly knotted.
the harder i pull
the more secure
in the trap
i become.
always fighting against what is
now i'm stuck,
immovable.
this isn't a sticky web
woven through creation,
through inspiration.
i'm not cocooning,
preparing for transformation
or rebirth.
this is a net
dragging the bottom of the ocean floor
and violently twisting around me.
this is no place for a human.

XVIII

i drew my own map,
riddled with expectations that i'm not sure were my own –
no deviating or bending.
no path home.

XIX

the child of my soul
looked with growing despair
while she drifted,
unprepared,
to the place where the water met the sky.

all alone,
in a ship with no sail,
in the middle of her world's most treacherous storm –
i didn't think i could reach her
so i didn't even try.

she deserved a departure from this life.
deserved to be cast
overboard,
then swallowed
by the waves.

and yet,
she deserved the safety and eternal rest
found only at the bottom of the deepest ocean,
hidden from prying eyes
and unwanted touch.

there is a peace that accompanies death
for the part that has been left
totally vulnerable
and ultimately
completely shattered.

2. the return

back when everything was still to come,
luck leaked out everywhere.
i gave my promise to the world,
and the world followed me here.

– rita dove

XX

please hold me
so i can tell my legs
they can rest.
i'm not sure if i deserve that kindness
but i need it.
i've walked for quite a distance –
seeking –
always seeking.
i'm just another wandering spirit
too invested in the destination.

XXI

there's uncertainty
within the confines
of your own body
as you try
and fail
to discern
what choice to make.
if only
someone would tell you
exactly what to do,
place you
on exactly the right road –
the one that leads
to what's best.
but there is no trust here
within yourself.
and no one else
has your answers.
they all have their
own unanswered questions
lurking below their own surfaces.
so you must be the one
to answer yourself.
gather your courage
and push aside
that persistent doubt
to reveal
your own strength
and to empower
your own knowing.

XXII

winter lingered in these bones
icy and brittle
ready to snap
if the wind blew too hard.
the thaw was slow
and painstaking.
the drip, drip, drip
of the melt
tormented the senses.
i needed to turn down the noise.
it was as if it was scraping at the inside of my mind.
i wanted to close my eyes
and sleep
deeply
in a space where
only the sweet chirping
of the returning birds
could wake me.

i wanted springtime
and the array of flowers that came with it.
but there would be no flowers
if i fell asleep and
failed to tend to the seeds.
winter still lingered
despite my resolve
but patience carried me through
to another season of new beginnings.
and eventually
i was warmed

from the inside out
by the sun
radiating
from deep within my body.

XXIII

i grabbed my fear by the neck and pulled.
ripping it from the earth
but the roots remained
down deep
fully nourished and secure
right where i had placed them so long ago,
right where i had tended to them so carefully,
right where i had protected them so fiercely.
i should plunge my hands deep into the soil
dig through the dirt until my hands bleed,
until i reach their lifelines.
but i'm tired of always having to get my hands dirty
just to undo
all that has been done.
i long to lie down
in a field of wildflowers
and drift off to sleep under the afternoon sun
while someone
else destroys the roots
of my deepest fears.
while someone else
takes care of it
so i can sleep
a dreamless
peaceful sleep.
one where i wake up in a new body.
a new life
with no memory of this one.
so i can start over
without anger,
without fear
without debilitating sadness and shame.

with just my beginner's mind
and my pure
untouched heart.
unaware and happy
to try again
this thing called life.

XXIV

the moment i let someone touch my scars
was the moment they began to fade.
they existed hidden and suffocated
under cotton sleeves,
anxious fingers always grasping at the fabric,
pulling it down to ensure they remained unseen.
i felt them burning brightly under the cover of my clothes –
a secret not many would try to understand.

nevertheless,
on a bitter night in the middle of winter
he ran his fingers over them,
tracing them gently.
an explanation sticking in my throat
unable to escape.
panicked and frozen.
but he just pulled me closer and drifted off to sleep.

morning came too soon as usual.
the sun was not yet up.
he brought me closer still
and there was a knowing –
no need to be ashamed.

it was then,
in the darkest, coldest season
that i stripped myself bare
and allowed a part of me to be uncovered.

XXV

how can i hurt myself?
the only question searing through my mind

a brain on fire
ready to burn the entire place down
fanning the flames
lighting more matches
destruction being the only goal

searching for weapons
for poison
for another way out
and i tear at my arms
nails like razor blades against my angry flesh

the temperature rising
sending chills up my spine
i'm on fire
but ice cold

then somehow
in the midst of it all
a pause.
a slight breath
a moment of silence
then a glimpse of clarity.

and i wonder –
maybe i've been asking myself the wrong question all along.

so
in that pause

that slight breath
that moment of silence
that glimpse of clarity
i ask...
what can i do to help myself?

and the fire begins to weaken.

XXVI

rest.
my biggest rebellion.

i shut my eyes in the most darkened room
trying to be unaware of the world around me,
my body
resisting waking.
my mind resisting sleep –

deep down just a child
trying to get a few more seconds
without judgment,
somehow forgetting
that i'm now allowed to choose.

there's a heaviness
in a sleep i feel i don't deserve,
a restlessness
that vibrates in the bones,
never allowing true rest.

incessant nagging from my mind
insisting i'm not doing enough.
and then the final decision,
a quiet revolution,
in closing the eyes
and letting it all go.

XXVII

there is so much more than this.
so hold on tight
to the threads you need,
the ones that keep you tethered.
they are not as flimsy and as weak as they appear.
a bit worn maybe,
as you've held them just like this
many times before.
their fibers welcome your grip
and your own hands only strengthen them.
though they appear fragile
they are unbreakable.

oh, there is so much more than this.
there is a love waiting for you
if you could only accept
that not everything has conditions
or needs something from you.
it is a love that has banished the idea of worthiness.
there is nothing to prove,
no one to be
except the person you are
right now
in this very moment.

know that there is so much more than this.
though it may feel impossible,
the possibilities are actually endless.
and the love that is waiting for you
is limitless
and without expectation,

without hesitation,
without restraint.
so surrender to the love that is beyond your own power
and know
there is so much more than this.

XXVIII

now is the time to let go.
look around you –
the earth is showing you the way.

the leaves do not cry out to the branches to hold them tightly
nor do the branches beg the leaves to stay.

just allow the natural rhythm of things to guide you,
without resistance,
into a new season of your own life.

observe the richness radiating from that naked forest
and know
that even when it seems you've lost it all,
there is still an aliveness,
a strong heartbeat sustaining and carrying you forward
until you can once again, as i know you will,
flourish and bloom.

XXIX

the mind refused to surrender
despite losing over and over again –
it didn't know
that surrender
was the only way to win.

the leaning in,
the feeling,
was the true path to freedom –

to breaking down all of the defenses
until nothing was left
but a pile of rubble
and a chance to rebuild.

XXX

i wondered –
who am i to open my mouth?
but then again . . .

i wanted to hear my own voice.
strong, steady
and sure.

i wanted to sing a song.
to allow the music to vibrate from my throat
and into the air.

i wanted to see how far the sound would carry.
i imagined it in my mind.
a beautiful, continuous melody traveling across the entire continent.

XXXI

and then the fog lifted.
this time all at once.
like a sharp inhale
allowing oxygen to flood my lungs.
i could see clearly again
and it all didn't look as bad as it once appeared.

XXXII

i left the shore
despite knowing
the riptide
was determined to drag me under
despite feeling
the slight tinge
of apprehension
and despite hearing
the voices of my past
saying what they've always said.

at first i carefully
deliberately
and strategically
stepped one foot
into the brilliant blue ocean
then
in a wild tantrum
of unbridled abandon
i fully entered
and allowed myself to be engulfed.

after diving
over and through the waves
after fighting the tides
and their relentless pursuit to drown me
all i felt was calm
as i had made it
beyond the ninth wave
to a place where
there was nothing left to fight against
and all of the treasure was mine.

XXXIII

ever present
for the moment.
the weight of it all
gently pressing down,
careful not to crush me
as it makes itself known.
"i'm here," it whispers
but i'm unsure how to respond
to the thing that has tried to kill me before.

i imagine it swaying above me,
held only by the thinnest chord
that threatens to break
and release its full weight upon me.
but i do not consent to that.
not now.
not today.
just for today
i will survive this.

and if tomorrow
the weight of it all
presses down more firmly,
i will survive that too
with full permission
to tend to myself
while i choose to remember
that this ever-present presence
is only temporary.

XXXIV

deep within me
i have had a yearning
for this sweet
soothing
soul rest.
where the rooms of my mind
are filled with an easy silence
creating safety
while i gently recline
into the sanctuary
of my own heart
to touch
an inner wisdom
long forgotten.

XXXV

i chose
to listen
to the alarm bells
warning
that the earth
was about to crumble
beneath me.
though i did not
rush to my feet
with urgency,
i did not ignore them either.
my body
felt as heavy
as twenty bodies
as i pulled myself up
slowly and with care.
i rose,
my legs
weak and unsteady
but able to hold me
all the same.
and they carried me away
to the safe house
of my heart
to rest
and to repair
the foundation of my soul.

please
do not let me forget myself.
when the voices rage
and i cannot hear my own thoughts,
help me remember
that i am good
and i am decent
even when there is a war inside of me
and all feels lost,
when through my eyes
the world seems grey
and dull.
please –
i cannot forget
that life is colorful,
vibrant
and real.
that i am real
and i am here –
for a purpose i cannot yet see
but one that is also unimaginably clear.

XXXVII

i loved myself today.
rather than running away
i greeted myself.
arms stretched wide open,
i embraced myself.
dulled the hurt through love.
i stopped shaming myself.
in using my breath,
i came back to myself.
through rest and ease
i comforted myself.
i allowed my tears to flow
and i cleansed myself.

such simple acts
yet they took so much courage.

XXXVIII

i am the ship and the captain.
the entire crew is every soul i've encountered along the way.
i am alone –
but i can feel them with me
as i lead myself to the arms of a new shore.

a storm came to sink me.
wave after wave
pushing me further from the shore.
how do i steer this ship,
one that is so poorly made and damaged from the long journey?
on my hands and knees i cry, then wrap my arms around my own body,
reaching, holding something that feels like hope, and i can clearly see
it's a vision or maybe even a dream
and that image bursts from my heart and i see it come to life.
before my eyes the storm is shifting around me –
the water is still.
i am a force field of protection.
i am powerful
though i am weary
but not as fragile as i once believed.

XL

the time for punishment is gone.
the tearing at your flesh and throwing of daggers at your own image
is finished.
too much time have you spent hiding yourself away
trying to repair something that was never broken.
the shame will destroy you.
the doubting and shrinking will gnaw at your heart.
and the heavy weight of the blame you've imposed upon yourself
will crush you.

but the time for punishment is gone.
and though you may long for it in the darkest of moments,
remember, it never had a purpose.
so, wrap your arms around your own body and weep.
for now is the time to finally comfort all that was hidden away.
the raging storm in your mind can rest,
allow for a tranquility to overtake you and transport you
to a new way of being.

because the time for punishment is gone.

XLI

take a few steps
backwards
to take it all in.
to see the whole
of what you've created –
an unfinished
but truly masterful
work of art.

look closely
at all you had been missing
while you stood within your life,
as you were meant to.
but now stand back
to examine the entirety
thus far.

how often
we miss all that has brought us here.
and as we strive and strive for more
we discount all we've already done,
minimizing our wisdom
time and time again,
forgetting all the life we've already lived.

XLII

digging through the scorched earth,
fingernails scraping the soil,
frantically trying to find a place safe enough
to lay these seeds to rest.

dry air and sweeping winds,
sand and dust blowing all around –
this was no place to bloom.

nothing could survive here
in the wild with no care or attention –
an abandoned desert
that hadn't seen rain in over a decade.
desolate and forgotten.

but still

it was my own hands
that raked through the dirt
to bury the seeds in a place where no one
would go looking.

and it was then that
i reclaimed the abandoned desert of my body
and tended to the seeds resting in the earth,
imagined them rooting in the place where nothing
before them had survived,
then cried as they pushed through the surface
and turned toward the sun.

XLIII

i'm ready to touch the reality.

that's the beauty of proximity,
of staying
up close
and uncomfortable –

to see the truth of a person
in all of their raw and messy wonder
instead of standing on the outskirts
where the perception is skewed.

oh,
the courage it takes
to breach the space
and live up close.

you are not stuck in the cycle.
even though
the pain feels immense.
this is different.
you are different.
even when the heaviness hangs over each moment
and it's hard to breathe
and the thoughts seem severe.
but this is not the spiral.
this will not be the end of you.
even though it seems like it should be.
the voice is loud
but you are louder
in your own quiet way.
there is no way you can falter
not while you're holding so much life in your hands.
let the heaviness linger.
breathe into the forgotten places
and allow yourself to cry.
you're allowed to cry.

exhale
and cry
knowing that you are not stuck here
and knowing that all of this heaviness
will not last forever.
the pain is so immense
as it has always been
but you are not lost in the spiral.
you are free –
freer than you've ever been
to be the most like you

you've ever been.
so be more,
more of you.
without apology
or fear
or judgment.
be wild,
as wild as you've ever dreamed to be,
wild as you were meant to be
and know
that you are not stuck here.

XLV

i lit a fire to illuminate the path
but there was no path before me.
only a child living in the shadows
in the middle of a quiet forest,
her eyes straining to catch a glimpse
of the life that she had been shut out of.
i rushed to take her into my arms
and carry her to safety
but she was not afraid,
she was not unsure.
on the contrary
she saw and knew
everything i had ever longed to see,
everything i had ever pretended to know.
and she took my hand,
leading me to a place only she could find
as there was no path
but she knew the way by heart.
the fire behind us grew
so as to light the way
while we raced through the trees.
she was laughing and singing,
unaware of my growing anxiety
about the unknown destination.
then
she asked me to sing with her
and in that forest
under the moonlit sky
i allowed my voice to match hers.
it was then i realized
she had brought me home.

XLVI

the brilliance of the sun on the water
was something to behold.
early morning air,
early morning sounds –
i can stay here,
totally still
for just another moment longer.
after all
what is the urgency?
there is none.
but i feel it still –
the quickening of the heart
urging me onward.
it always feels as if i'm running out of time
even when there's nowhere to be.
i'm always racing
towards an arbitrary finish line,
hoping
to find satisfaction within myself
after i cross it.

perhaps the satisfaction lies within the witnessing
of the sun on the water
or feeling the salty breeze on my face
or hearing the sounds of the birds calling from the sky.
maybe it's within the stopping,
the sitting,
the seeing
and the stillness –
the "just being."
i'm coming to realize that is enough.

and if that is enough
maybe i am enough
and not required
to prove anything.
i exist
as the sun exists,
as the wind exists,
as the birds exist.
and that is enough.

acknowledgments

A deep bow of gratitude to each and every person who has loved and supported me on this journey back to the true self.

To all of my family and friends who have encouraged me to show myself and have helped me feel confident enough to even dream of creating this collection, thank you. Thank you for always being excited and willing to read my work. Thank you for listening and for calming my anxieties when I felt unsure. And thank you for allowing me the space to learn and grow.

To Pasha, who, a little over a year ago, planted the seed in my mind that blossomed into this collection: I appreciate you more than you know. Thank you for opening my heart to the idea and for believing in me.

To my husband, Guy, for always making me feel safe and fully supported and for always encouraging me to chase my dreams: I couldn't have created this without you. You make me feel that I can do anything I set my mind to. I love you more than words can say.

And to you, the reader, for giving these words a place to live: I appreciate you so much. I hope you find comfort in these pages.

I am grateful beyond measure.

about the author

Caitlin Blackburn is a Reiki Master/Teacher, poet, and licensed social worker from Niantic, Connecticut. Though she has been writing since she was a child, this is her first published body of work. Poetry has always served as a source of comfort and inspiration for her, and her hope is that this collection will offer that to others.

This book is set in Garamond Premier Pro, which had its genesis in 1988 when type-designer Robert Slimbach visited the Plantin-Moretus Museum in Antwerp, Belgium, to study its collection of Claude Garamond's metal punches and typefaces. During the 1500s Garamond – a Parisian punch-cutter – produced a refined array of book types that combined an unprecedented degree of balance and elegance, for centuries standing as the pinnacle of beauty and practicality in type-founding. They were based on the handwriting of Angelo Vergecio, court librarian of the French king, Francis I. Slimbach has created a new interpretation based on Garamond's designs and on compatible italics cut by Robert Granjon, Garamond's contemporary.

Copies of this book can be ordered
from all bookstores including Amazon
or directly from the author
by contacting her via
cablackburn3@gmail.com.

•

For more information on the work of Caitlin Blackburn,
visit www.antrimhousebooks.com/authors.html.

CPSIA information can be obtained
at www.ICGtesting.com
Printed in the USA
LVHW111651120223
739300LV00006B/279